Destined

for

FAITH

MARTY DELMON

DESTINED FOR FAITH
Marty Delmon

Published by:
RPJ & COMPANY, INC.
P.O. Box 160243 | Altamonte Springs, FL 32716-0243 | 407.551.0734
www.rpjandco.com

ISBN-13: 978-0-9819980-4-6
ISBN-10: 0-98199804-6

Cover Image:
© bruno magnien - Fotolia.com

Cover Design Concept: Marty Delmon

Cover & Interior Design:
Kathleen Schubitz
RPJ & COMPANY, INC.
www.rpjandco.com

Scripture quote on cover: Matthew 17:20, KJV

Printed in the United States of America.

Destined

for

FAITH

RPJ & Company, Inc.

www.rpjandco.com

Table of Contents

TRUST AND OBEY

My first baby steps in faith started when someone put a cassette in my hand entitled "You Can Have Anything You Want from God as Long as You Can Find It in the Bible." Now I may have elongated that title a bit but that's in essence what it said. When I received that tape, I was ready to receive.

I thought it over and decided what I wanted from God. I wanted to be a millionaire. I'd never been one of those, so I looked in the Word to see if I could be that. The word 'millionaire' doesn't appear in the Bible, but extraordinary wealth certainly does. Consider Abraham, Isaac and Jacob. Consider Joseph who became second to Pharaoh. Consider the Israelites when they left Egypt carrying the wealth of the Egyptians with them. Consider the booty the Israeli armies took throughout the Old Testament. Consider Solomon! He heaped silver in piles in the city because he had so much! The Queen of Sheba traveled to Israel to see for herself all the rumors of his wealth and the rumors proved to be *less* than reality!

> *Now all these things happened to them as examples, and they were written for our admonition, upon whom the ends of the ages have come (1 Corinthians 10:11).*

The things written in the Old Testament give examples for us who live under the New Testament. Born again Christians are heirs of Abraham to whom was given the promise and the experience of great wealth. We've inherited that same promise. Great wealth is a blessing from God for His children. So let's look at this promise given to Abraham.

> *After these things the word of the Lord came to Abram in a vision, saying, "Do not be afraid, Abram. I am your shield, your exceedingly great reward" (Genesis 15:1).*

Okay, okay, I hear you. That blessing was for Abraham, but I'm living here in the 21st century and what does that blessing mean to me?

> *...The blessing of Abraham might come upon the Gentiles in Christ Jesus, that we might receive the promise of the Spirit through faith (Galatians 3:14).*

And if you are Christ's, then you are Abraham's seed, and heirs according to the promise (Galatians 3:29).

Abraham believed God and received the blessing. As his seed, help yourself, as we Americans say at the dinner table. Believe God and receive the blessing. What is the blessing?

The blessing of the Lord makes one rich, and He adds no sorrow with it (Proverbs 10:22).

Trust me. I am NOT saying that the people with great wealth have it because God blessed them with it. There are two ways to get wealth in today's society: by worldly means and by godly means. We know all about the ones with worldly wealth as they are lavishly praised in periodicals or flaunted on TV. In the Christian world many people who serve God also have great wealth; we just don't read about them in *The New York Times*.

And I thank Christ Jesus our Lord who has enabled me, because He counted me faithful… (1 Timothy 1:12).

This verse goes on to say God enabled Paul to go into the ministry, but don't think that leaves you out. God enables all His children, not just His ministers. I understood that if I wanted to be a millionaire I would have to be faithful to that concept. I would have to hold that thought perpetually in my being: in my mind, in my emotions, in my will and in my body. The promise already lived in my spirit as that's where the Holy Spirit resides and He knows that great wealth belongs to me. I also realized that under no circumstances could I doubt my status of millionaire.

> **But let him ask in faith, with no doubting, for he who doubts is like a wave of the sea driven and tossed by the wind. For let not that man suppose that he will receive anything from the Lord; he is a double-minded man, unstable in all his ways (James 1:6-8).**

In order to hold that thought perpetually before me, I wrote on 3 x 5 cards all the Scriptures I could find about the promise of wealth, personalizing them with first person pronouns and even with my name. I plastered those cards all over the house and in my car. If I combed my hair while looking in the mirror, a card stared at me from the very center of my sight pattern. If I pulled down the sunshade while driving, there was a card. If I opened a cupboard for a water glass, a card hung from the shelf holding the glass. If I unrolled toilet paper, there was a Scripture right above the roll.

When doubt crept in I had to start all over, asking the Lord's forgiveness for doubt and unbelief – those are the only two elements that cause faith not to work. Then I restated my request to be a millionaire. It does not bother God how many times we start again. Of course He would prefer that we establish our faith and stick with it the first time; but we are free to start again with Him as often as it takes for us to build up to unquestionable faith.

> ***The steps of a good man are ordered by the LORD, and He delights in his way. Though he fall, he shall not be utterly cast down; for the LORD upholds him with His hand (Psalm 37:23-24).***

Some people, when they fall, think it's all over. They've failed God and that's that. But it's never "that's that" with God. He always picks us up and upholds us in His hand. Sometimes people try to put time limits on God, like "If I don't receive it by May 10th then it's all over. I've failed." God's timing is not our timing. As the saying goes, "He's never late, but He's never early. He's always right on time." That's about the best timing you can place on God – *thank You for never being late.* Give it up. He's in control and He wants you to have your heart's desire.

During the time I believed God to be a millionaire, my former husband came home from work every day with this proclamation. "We're going to lose everything! We're headed for the poorhouse!" I learned not to argue with him as that made him even more determined he was right. I learned not to agree with him as that broke my covenant with the Lord.

Instead I trained myself to run into the other room and pray. "Father, forgive him. He doesn't know what he's saying. You and I have a covenant that I will believe You and You will provide. I am believing You for one million dollars and I will not break my belief. Because of Your Word I know You will supply."

On some of my cards I even wrote things like: "God is bringing me one million dollars."

My former husband sat me down and said, "Remove that card! You can't say that. There is no chance in hell we're getting one million dollars! In our position in life it just isn't possible. Can you see any way for us to get it?"

I'd say something mild like, "Only in God," which would set him off ranting at me again.

Miraculously, he did not take my cards down. With great disgust he left me in my folly. He knew he could do that because my sister stood on his side. She said, very gently, "Marty, people are going to think you are a fool. Please, you're embarrassing your family; be sensible. Those who have a million dollars are people who have worked for it." In a worldly sense I knew she was right, but in a godly sense I knew God promises wealth, not from the toil of our hands but from our trust and our obedience.

> *Therefore do not cast away your confidence, which has great reward. For you have need of endurance, so that after you have done the will of God, you may receive the promise: (Hebrews 10:35-36).*

Notice when this verse says you will receive the promise of God (for whatever you are believing Him to produce, be it a job, a mate, wealth, health, or any of the other 7,000 promises in the Bible). It says you will receive it AFTER you have done the will of God. That's the obedience part. Obeying what He says or even whispers or maybe nudges on the inside of you; that's the key.

I started this faith walk to become a millionaire in 1982 and over a period of three years I experienced many testings. Like every Christian, I had to learn obedience through a learning-curve - just like in school. We learn a lot more when we know we're going to be tested. Always remember that the testing is for our edification, not to bring God up to speed on our progress. He already knows.

God wrote the story of Abraham's life in the Bible as an explicit example to us of what to do and what not to do in our walk of faith. Let's take a look at a certain testing period he went through. In Genesis 12:1-7 God told Abraham what He would do for him. We call this a promise. He said the words and then, after some time passed, He did what He said He would do.

> ... *"Get out of your country, from your family and from your father's house, to a land that I will show you. I will make you a great nation; I will bless you and make your name great; and you shall be a blessing. I will bless those who bless you, and I will curse him who curses you; and in you all the families of the earth shall be blessed" (V 1-3).*

That encapsulated part one. Abraham did most of it. He took Sarah and left, following the leading of the Lord to the land of Canaan, but he failed when he took Lot with him. And the descendants of Lot, still today, behave like a thorn in Abraham's side. When they arrived in Canaan in Shechem under the terebinth tree God gave another portion of the promise.

> *...To your descendants I will give this land (V 7).*

Then we continue to read about his life for a couple of chapters. We see what he decided to do about having a beautiful wife while they were in Egypt. We read the story of Lot and how he took the best land. Lot gets captured during a war and Abraham doesn't stop to question whether or not he should save this greedy nephew, he simply goes after him. The King offered Abraham the spoil from the war and surprise, surprise, Abraham declined the offer.

After all that drama we read this sentence: *After these things the word of the Lord came to Abram in a vision, saying, "Do not be afraid, Abram. I am your shield, your exceedingly great reward" (Genesis 15:1).*

When I read the Bible I like to question things. After all, the One who wrote it lives inside me so I can get my understanding directly from The Source. I wanted to know: why did God say *"after these things...?"* Shouldn't He have spoken these words right after He gave the promise? Why speak this out three chapters later?

Then I realized Abraham was being tested and he did not score 100%. (Makes you feel better about your own test score, doesn't it?) Since the promise was to Abraham and his descendants, he had to assume God would save his wife. In this series of tests, Abraham flunked the first one. He told Sarah that when the Egyptians saw her beauty they would kill him to get her.

Now if I were God listening to this conversation, (because He not only listens, He knows what we're going to say before we say it), I'd think Abraham hadn't believed my promise. What happened to his faith in what God said? Great nation, great name, and Abraham speaks about death, about being killed. What kind of faith is that? God's faith, however, never fails, so He turned it all for good and Abraham walked out of Egypt a rich man. God has unfailing faith in you as well.

Next, if God intended to make him into a great nation, then Abraham didn't need to grab the best land. Lot could take it. This seems puzzling since the Lord promised Abraham the land that Lot took. However, Abraham passed the second test as he trusted that God would do what He said He would do without Abraham meddling with the contract. Lot lost the land.

Now about Abraham rescuing Lot, if God said He would make his name great, didn't Abraham have to do his part by putting his faith to work? How can anyone have a great name if he just sits around and doesn't give a helping hand, especially to a family member? Abraham knew God would give him success in bringing Lot home.

And finally, the King offered Abraham the spoil of the war and Abraham declined because God said He would make him great. He said to the King, *...I have raised my hand to the Lord, God Most High, the Possessor of heaven and earth, that I will take nothing, from a thread to a sandal strap, and that I will not take anything that is yours, lest you should say, 'I have made Abram rich'– (Genesis 14:22-23).*

Abraham passed the majority of these tests. He believed the promise and acted on it. He grew in faith through each one of these experiences.

> *...That the genuineness of your faith, being much more precious than gold that perishes, though it is tested by fire, may be found to praise, honor, and glory at the revelation of Jesus Christ (1 Peter 1:7).*

The major benefit in faith is huge! Something dynamic comes from the spirit realm where God the Father, Jesus the Son and Holy Spirit the guide all live. The thing you asked for which does not yet exist on this earth, at least not in your life, that only exists in heaven, comes down. That dynamic something expresses itself in the natural realm where we humans live. Before, heaven kept it in store and now, it resides on earth. God wants to change our world through our faith. That's what makes Him happy.

There is an erroneous saying that I used to believe until I realized it's unbiblical even though it carries an element of truth: "God is happiest when His children are at play." God enjoys our joy. The Bible says Jesus was the most glad of all his fellows and our Father wants us to be glad or full of joy as well. But if we want to make God happy, we will walk in faith.

> *Now the just shall live by faith; but if anyone draws back, My soul has no pleasure in him"* (*Hebrews 10:38*).

> *But without faith it is impossible to please Him, for he who comes to God must believe that He is, and that He is a rewarder of those who diligently seek Him* (*Hebrews 11:6*).

Faith is a two step process. The first step is Trust and the second step is Obedience. What does it mean "to trust"? To understand that word we have to understand exactly what Jesus did for us and to do that we have to go back to Adam. The mystery begins here.

God gave Adam and Eve everything they could possibly want. They lived in a beautiful garden. It contained every plant, every flower, every vegetable God had created. It contained every animal God had made and, incredibly, they all lived in peace. Plus, Adam got to name all those animals. I've always wanted to pet a polar bear; haven't you? Adam and Eve got to romp and play with these magnificent animals!

In the garden the temperature was so perfect they did not need to wear clothes. Their souls were so perfect they had no shame; in fact, they were covered with the Glory of God so they didn't realize they were naked. Their minds were so perfect they could walk and talk with God every day and not stutter for words while conversing with the Omniscient One. Their emotions were so perfect they lived in love and joy all the time with no disagreements, no struggle for control as there was no sense of superiority or inferiority.

But they lost it all when they picked that one fruit from the Tree of Knowledge of Good and Evil. Everything they had before eating that fruit was Good; but now they introduced Evil into their lives and they lost their garden. They were sent to live where weeds grew between the plants; the ground hardened; certain flora produced thorns. The animals developed animosity toward one another; some became carnivores and they all separated themselves from Adam and Eve, no longer trusting them.

Instead of freely finding food, Adam had to work by the sweat of his labor. Eve had to give birth to children through great pain. Adam became macho overnight. Eve chased after him like an underling. Unrestricted love converted into conditional love. Joy turned elusive. They both hid from God when He came to walk and talk with them as they found themselves to be insufficient. The Glory left.

God cannot be found at fault here as He warned them, *And the Lord God commanded the man, saying, "Of every tree of the garden you may freely eat; but of the tree of the knowledge of good and evil you shall not eat, for in the day that you eat of it you shall surely die" (Genesis 2:16-17).*

We have been dying in every sense of the word since Adam and Eve made that decision to cheat on the Lord. Even though nothing was intended to die, everything does. We needed a Savior to save us from eternal death because we certainly couldn't do it ourselves. Jesus came, conquered death and set us free. He is called the Second Adam.

> *For as in Adam all die, even so in Christ all shall be made alive (1 Corinthians 15:22).*
>
> *And so it is written, "The first man Adam became a living being." The last Adam became a life-giving spirit. However, the spiritual is not first, but the natural, and afterward the spiritual. The first man was of the earth, made of dust, the second Man is the Lord from heaven. As was the man of dust, so also are those who are made of dust; and as is the heavenly Man, so also are those who are heavenly. And as we have borne the image of the man of dust, we shall also bear the image of the heavenly Man (1 Corinthians 15:45-49).*

So what did Jesus do about all that Adam lost for us? He gave His Body and His Blood as perfect payment for every sickness and every sin. We say glibly that He bought us back. That has a certain cash register ring to it. It was not a cut and dried occasion. With passion he wrested us from the clutches of the enemy and restored us to the loving possession of our Father God. He who loves us beyond comprehension now has us back in His arms.

Jesus came to restore the Garden of Eden, that idyllic existence, that special relationship with God that Adam lost for us by his decision to disobey the Almighty. Only now it is a little more complicated. Jesus had to pay with His Blood to purchase us back. What's more, He had to leave us here in this negative atmosphere until Adam's physical time ends.

However, Jesus did restore that garden, gave us an idyllic existence and the ability to walk and talk with God our Father any time we want! All of this is established and waiting for us on the spiritual level. It is by faith that we draw it down into our natural, physical life. God doesn't just want us to have "Pie in the Sky!" He wants us to have "Steak on our Plate!" Only faith can bring that to pass. This takes a profound level of trust that is not for the lukewarm. It's an *all or nothing* faith. Sure you can do it. It's just a matter of answering this question: *Do you want it bad enough?*

Trust means to believe on the name of the Lord Jesus Christ to the outrageous extent that we believe He will deliver everything we want and need right into our hands. Trust is total surrender. Trust worries about nothing. The Lord tells us over and over in the New Testament to become like little children, which means what? It means to trust like a little child trusts its parents to give it food, clothing and shelter. Do you ever see a little child, say two years old, worrying about its future? Of course not, a child naturally trusts. God wants child-like trust in Him to be found in us.

> **And this is His commandment: that we should believe on the name of His son Jesus Christ and love one another, as He gave us commandment (1 John 3:23).**

What does that mean; we should believe on the name of His son Jesus Christ? I puzzled over this a lot in the beginning. Am I supposed to believe that His name is Jesus Christ? That's a little too simplistic even for the Bible. What does believing on a name mean? A name carries the person with it, doesn't it? In this case the person behind the name is the Son of the Living God, meaning He is everything God is. No matter what attribute, gift or grace God has, His Son is also endowed with it. He is God.

Now if you believe that Jesus, who is your Lord by your new birth, has every power and every authority of God, then you will believe that His name has the same power and authority. If you happen to be a Christian did you also happen to notice that you carry His name? Christ-ian. This may be a leap of faith for you, but if you carry His name then you have all the power and authority He has. Is there any lack in Jesus? Is there any lack in God? Of course not. What does that ultimately mean? There is no lack in you.

You are in Jesus and He is in you. You are in the Holy Spirit and He is in you. God Himself has come to live inside you. That is the mystery of the ages.

> *... Christ in you, the hope of glory (1 Colossians 1:27b).*

Believe in that. Trust that. Have faith. Learn to live in that victory. You have a domain that you rule – your world – and all the power to rule that world is in you. You overcome your world with your faith.

> **For this is the love of God, that we keep His commandment. And His commandments are not burdensome. For whatever is born of God overcomes the world. And this is the victory that has overcome the world – our faith. Who is he who overcomes the world, but he who believes that Jesus is the Son of God? (1 John 5:3-5).**

Easy? Did I say faith was easy? Not on your life! It is the only fight mentioned in the New Testament. We no longer kill our enemies. We no longer fight for position. Let's face it, Christianity is not violent. I don't care how many legions of soldiers have gone to war for the glory of God, they were not sent to the battlefield by Jesus. Now defense is another story. Every ruler has the obligation to protect his or her people from evil.

> **For rulers are not a terror to good works, but to evil. Do you want to be unafraid of the authority? Do what is good, and you will have praise from the same. For he is God's minister to you for good. But if you do evil, be afraid; for he does not bear the sword in vain; for he is**

> **God's minister, an avenger to execute wrath on
> him who practices evil (Romans 13:3-4).**

However, there is one battle we must wage offensively and defensively, and that's the fight of faith. Sometimes faith is easy. If you've been believing God to give you a nice sunny day for your birthday picnic and there hasn't been a drop of rain in a week and none are forecast by the weather channel, hey! Piece of cake! But if your child has been diagnosed with a terminal disease and the medical profession gives you no hope whatsoever, faith becomes a major battle, totally winnable, but a battle.

> **Fight the good fight of faith, lay hold on eternal
> life, to which you were also called and have
> confessed the good confession in the presence of
> many witnesses (1 Timothy 6:12).**

Faith doesn't quit even when everything looks like it's not going to happen. Faith perseveres in the face of all adversity. Every single person in your sphere of influence can be telling you to give up, it's a lost cause, but your faith will smile and shake your head no. You know that you know that you know you will win in the end because God gave you faith to be your servant and to accomplish for you whatever He has promised! Notice how Jesus teaches the apostles about faith.

> **And the apostles said to the Lord, "Increase our
> faith." So the Lord said, "If you have faith as a
> mustard seed, you can say to this mulberry tree,**

'Be pulled up by the roots and be planted in the sea,' and it would obey you. And which of you, having a servant plowing or tending sheep, will say to him when he has come in from the field, 'Come at once and sit down to eat'? But will he not rather say to him, 'Prepare something for my supper, and gird yourself and serve me till I have eaten and drunk, and afterward you will eat and drink'? Does he thank that servant because he did the things that were commanded him? I think not. So likewise you, when you have done all those things which you are commanded, say, 'We are unprofitable servants. We have done what was our duty to do'" (Luke 17:5-10).

Now honestly, pause here for a moment. Jesus answered the apostles' question about increasing their faith by telling them a story about service. What's that all about? Consider. Is the servant, by any chance, the faith they are asking about? Is Jesus saying to them, "Keep your faith working and expect it to do what you demand and you will see it accomplish the task you give it?" He ends the discussion by showing them that when God asks them to do something they simply do it. Likewise the servant named Faith when it is put to work will simply do what you've asked it to do.

So if Jesus gave us this divine seed of faith at the moment of our new birth, then we'd better learn how to put it to work as our servant. The only things faith can work on are heavenly things; that's where faith comes from. The only way you will know which tasks to put your faith to work on is by reading the Bible, the very words of God, the heavenly manual. Faith is your divine servant. You order your servant to do for you what the Bible tells you is available.

> ***So then faith comes by hearing, and hearing by the word of God (Romans 10:17).***

Some friends of mine did something very, very stupid in my opinion. Their son disappeared. He warned them he intended to drop out of college, get high, stay high and sure enough, he did. My friends asked the Pastor of their church to form a prayer group to stand in faith that their son would come home and choose to live for the Lord instead of the life he had chosen. They said they could not be a part of the group. They were going to surrender to worrying, fretting, and thinking of all the bad things that could happen to their son. They knew they couldn't help but be depressed so someone else would have to carry the faith load.

Other Christians are our fellow workers, but they can't do the job for us. Each Christian has a direct line to God; there is no intermediary. I've had other Christians pray for me a lot, but their prayers only work when my faith is joined to theirs. I like the analysis of the California Redwood Tree. Those huge, tall trees with those strong, solid trunks, even though they are 100s of feet tall, have tiny little roots. What holds them up? They grow in stands, clumped together, and they wrap their roots around each other. That's why when one dies it takes dozens of years for it to finally fall to the ground because the little roots are holding on so tightly.

Christians are like that. We cling together, praying for each other, holding each other up. But if the one needing the prayer doesn't participate, the others can hold on and hold on, but eventually the needy one will fall. You have to stand in faith. You have to walk in faith. The last I heard my friends' son still wasn't clean and that's 20 long years of parental nightmares.

> **Not that we have dominion over your faith, but are fellow workers for your joy; for by faith you stand (2 Corinthians 1:24).**

Who stands in faith? Your friends? Your Pastor? You stand. They are fellow workers with you. Nothing is stronger than joined faith; that's why joining in prayer is the greatest gift you can give. I tried to explain this to my friends and she said, "Oh no. When I wake up at night terrified about what might be happening to my son, I know someone else is standing in faith and I can cry myself back to sleep." I hope you can see the absurdity of her position. By faith you stand.

Every once in a while I like to ask the Lord what does not please Him about me and every time He has an answer right on His lips and it's usually the same kind of response. Just once I'd like it if He'd pause and say, "Let me think." But no. He instantly tells me, "You spend too much time with my enemy." I also know instantly what He means. I worry. Even a little bit of worry is too much. It's sin.

> **Do you have faith? Have it to yourself before God. Happy is the person who is free of self-**

condemnation when he has faith for something!
He who doubts is condemned, because he does
not act from faith; for whatever is not from faith
is sin. (*A composite of translations of Romans*
14:22-23).

Through my travels to so many different churches, I find I run into the same phenomenon everywhere: Christians who are doing nothing but sitting around and waiting. Sometimes they aren't even working! They either live on the dole from the government or from Christian agencies. When I ask them what they are doing they respond they are living by faith, or sometimes they say they are waiting on God. I honestly want to scream, "What are you thinking?"

Trusting God means to behave as if you trust Him and that means you are actively involved in the thing you are believing Him to do. For instance I believed for Him to make me a millionaire. What do millionaires do? I thought of the millionaires I've known and one thing became obvious. They give. One fellow who owned his own company, took a bunch of my friends out for a big dinner, there were like 20 of us. He opened his house for me to use for ministry purposes and we had some great meetings there,

I talked this over with the Lord. "I know I've got to start acting like a millionaire in order to be one, but I can't afford the extravagant giving." The Lord told me to start with what I have. I realized I couldn't send people to fine weekends at resorts like some had treated me, but I had a nice house and I could invite certain ones to come for a weekend in my home and pretend it was a bed and breakfast hotel.

While waiting for my million, I invited people that the Lord indicated to me to spend a weekend with us. I waited on my guests hand and foot, serving meals as if they were in a hotel, letting them have the privacy to lounge around my pool without being bothered, except to serve them cold drinks. I know they were blessed, but let me tell you who was the most blessed. Me! It really is more blessed to give than to receive.

I opened my home for Friday night meetings, inviting whatever traveling speaker who happened to be in the area to speak to the group. We had some awesome services! People drove for two or three hours to get to my Friday night meetings. I used my home for parties and dinners, inviting people who could not return the invitation. It became such a joy to give like this that I reached a point where I didn't care if the million came or not! But come it did.

Rich people liked to put money in my hands. So I started putting money in other people's hands. I've also noticed that millionaires don't always like to take the credit for the nice things they do. They do them anonymously. One time I put some money in a woman's purse which was lying open. She couldn't get over it. She squealed and squealed for what seemed like hours; she was so happy. Part of her excitement came from not knowing who did it.

I've made other certain specific gifts in which I've told the finance officer not to let anyone know it was me. The joy the people express thrills me. I discovered by doing these things that millionaires, at least Christian millionaires, have a lot of fun with their money, and I'm not talking about spending it on themselves. Giving is a lot of fun!

So you've got to work your faith, acting like you already have what you've asked for. The brother of Jesus, James, had a pretty good understanding of this faith/works principle.

> *What does it profit, my brethren, if someone says he has faith but does not have works? Can faith save him? (James 2:14).*

> *Thus also faith by itself, if it does not have works, is dead (James 2:17).*

> *But someone will say, "You have faith, and I have works." Show me your faith without your works, and I will show you my faith by my works (James 2:18).*

> *But do you want to know, O foolish man, that faith without works is dead? (James 2:20).*

> *Do you see that faith was working together with his works, and by works faith was made perfect? (James 2:22).*

> **You see then that a man is justified by works, and not by faith only (James 2:24).**

> **For as the body without the spirit is dead, so faith without works is dead also. (James 2:26).**

So let's wind this up. What is faith exactly? It is absolute trust in God the Father, Jesus the Son and Holy Spirit, our guide.

> **Examine yourselves as to whether you are in the faith. Test yourselves. Do you not know yourselves, that Jesus Christ is in you?... (2 Corinthians 13:5).**

If you know Jesus is in you, why bother dickering between His point of view – absolute victory – and the view of the world – absolute failure. I know, it's a simple choice when I put it like that. It's when circumstances stack up against you and Satan's lies bunch around your ears that the choice doesn't seem so obvious. Therefore choose. Choose before the choice becomes difficult. Will you or will you not trust God to take care of everything? Will you or will you not behave as if He has already done it?

Will you say with Paul: **I have fought the good fight, I have finished the race, I have kept the faith (2 Timothy 4:7).**

A STARTLING
ANSWER TO MY FAITH

For three years I learned to trust God for a seemingly impossible request, one million dollars, and I learned to obey Him with whatever appeal He made of me. Some of His requests made me gasp at what appeared to be their enormity but which, with His help, became easily manageable. I tried using my imagination during that trial period as to how God would provide me with one million dollars. Let me assure you, how He answered me and how He will answer you is beyond anything you can imagine.

One morning at 5 a.m. the phone rang. Groggy, my husband answered, got out of bed with the receiver and went into the other room. I could hear him asking over and over, "What?" "What did you say?" And I knew his brother was dead.

His brother was a man who lived on the edge. Any good church goer would call his life a life of sin. Let's just say he challenged the law and lived on the other side of it. The thing about sin is that from the foundations of the earth God wrote into the universe consequences for sin. It's not that God has to point His finger today and pass judgment on us. Our actions determine the judgment or the blessing that will follow them. Sin naturally has consequences that consistently tag along. Bear that in mind as I relate this story. It was not God who caused these circumstances; it was sin. As the Scriptures say, He made it turn for our good.

> *And we know that all things work together for good to those who love God, to those who are the called according to His purpose (Romans 8:28).*

Months before that early morning phone call, really curious as to how God would meet my faith I asked: "How are we going to get the money?" In a vision I saw our commissary as if I were standing across the street. For our business we had taken an old house and converted the street level, or the garage and downstairs rooms, into a commercial kitchen which serviced our four restaurants. We used the upstairs rooms for offices. The double wide garage door stood open and many policemen were coming in and out, measuring and making notes. Then out of the wrought iron gate several men wheeled a gurney with my brother-in-law's body on it completely covered by a white sheet.

I puzzled over this for weeks. My brother-in-law was way too young and healthy to die of a heart attack. How could he possibly die in the commissary? And how would that make us millionaires? It made no sense.

So I went back and asked Jesus, "When is my brother-in-law going to die?" He said, "On a holiday; on a Monday." Then He showed me two funerals going on side by side. The first one was my husband's brother's funeral and their mother was the second.

My brother-in-law's funeral made no sense to me. There was nothing wrong with him. And his mother would soon be 80. Shouldn't she die first? I told the Lord, "This isn't right. A mother should die before her son." But the positioning of the funerals did not change, so when the call came at 5 a.m., on Memorial Day, a holiday, a Monday, the Lord had forewarned me.

We owned four restaurants and a central kitchen where we prepared all the food. Small crews worked best in our cramped workspace so we scheduled kitchen crews the full 24 hours in a day. At 4 a.m. on this particular day the pastry chef came to work as usual. He had his own key to open the wrought iron gate at the sidewalk and come down the long, dark alley to unlock the door to the kitchen. He opened the door to find two dead bodies on the cement floor, laying in their blood, having been shot to death.

He called the police who arrived within minutes. They called my husband's sister-in-law and she immediately drove to the kitchen to identify the bodies. She told the police that someone had called from the commissary about midnight for her husband to come and fix the boiler. That boiler was a constant problem so she thought nothing of it and went to sleep without waiting for him and therefore didn't notice that he didn't come home.

One of the bodies was her husband. The other was a substitute cook. He had previously worked for us and knowing that our regular nighttime cook took a vacation that week, over Memorial Day, had asked if he could work that particular shift. Had he not worked my husband would have been on duty and maybe even me as I usually helped him when he covered for kitchen employees on vacation.

However, I think the plot would have been postponed if my husband had said no to the previous employee. The police said the two dead men were involved in selling and/or transporting drugs and circumstances made it seem like a drug deal gone wrong. They were referring to the fifty pound sacks of flour and white sugar that had been cut open and the contents strewn over the kitchen. An obvious hiding place for cocaine.

The replacement cook's girlfriend came to the wrought iron gate about 2 a.m. The cook came to talk to her at the gate but wouldn't let her in. He said things were really getting hot and he was afraid for her safety. She reported hearing voices shouting, the sound coming from the kitchen.

The police believed there were two killers. They made the men kneel, put their hands behind their backs, tied them with leather thongs and shot them in their backs underneath their shoulder blades. The bullets went directly into their hearts. They untied their wrists so no trace was left to implicate the killers, a very professional kill. The men died instantly and the police could not tell us which man was shot first.

My husband, when he arrived at work, was not allowed into the kitchen until the police were finished with their analysis. He stood on the sidewalk across the street and watched the police wheel his brother out on a gurney, his body completely covered by a white sheet. Then they brought him inside to question him. After the police left his sister-in-law came back to the commissary and cleaned out her husband's desk taking all his personal effects.

The minute my husband's brother died, the restaurants became vulnerable. We had a loan for $250,000 on the property which became due and payable at the moment of a partner's death. There were three partners, my husband had 22.5%, another man had 22.5% and my husband's brother had 55%. Neither the other partner nor we could come up with $250,000!

Had either of the other partners died, my brother-in-law could easily have obtained the necessary money. So my husband, who was the General Manager of the restaurants, had taken out an insurance policy on each partner's life to cover the estate of any partner and the note on the restaurants. My brother-in-law's policy amounted to one million dollars, $700,000 for his share of the restaurants and $300,000 to cover the note and whatever else might need to be paid. His children, not understanding the business ramifications of the insurance policies, instantly took out a law suit against us in order to obtain the full million dollars. The insurance company refused to pay the policy until the court decided who should get the money.

The bankruptcy my husband kept predicting loomed as the bank was leaning on us for the $250,000. The day came for the first court hearing and my husband was so depressed! We had no way of proving that the brother-in-law's share was $700,000 because all of his paperwork had been taken away by his wife and she was part of the law suit to obtain the million dollars.

But I had not given up on my faith! I was still doing my Faith Walk! Every day I claimed my million dollars and thanked God profusely for it. I read my Scriptures over and over inserting my name and praising God for such a blessing. So I was not surprised when on the day of the court date my husband idly opened a drawer in his brother's empty desk and found a sheet of paper. He had opened that same drawer dozens of times and always found it empty. On the paper, in my brother-in-law's handwriting, were these words: "My share of the restaurants is $700,000." An application for a loan was attached and on that paper he described the assets that would back the loan.

Where did that paper come from? I believe the Lord had it stick to the underneath of the desk top when the sister-in-law cleaned out the desk. Even when my husband kept opening the drawer in hope against hope that he would find something, anything, to help him out of the mess he was in, that paper clung to the roof of the drawer. But the very day we needed it, God caused it to float down to the bottom of the drawer where my husband could find it.

When he presented the paper to the judge later that morning, the judge denied the law suit and awarded the insurance money to the restaurants. By that afternoon the estate had been paid $700,000 and the note on the restaurants for $250,000 had been paid. Now we became 50% owners of our four restaurants and commissary. We put the restaurants up for sale; suddenly the real estate market bounced up and we made our million dollars. Like I said, I could never have imagined this scenario for receiving the money for which I stood in faith.

God knew the scenario was coming, however. When I get to heaven I'm going to ask Him if He planted that desire to be a millionaire in my heart. Perhaps He was helping me to overcome a plot the enemy devised against my family. Whatever the reason, it was now an accomplished fact.

As to the surprising sale of the restaurants, did the Lord make the market go up rapidly just for our benefit? I believe He did. One other time I had such an experience. I was scheduled to speak in a small church that did not have the funds to put me in a hotel, especially since my husband and two children were with me. Nor did the Pastor have a large enough home to accommodate us. So he asked a member of his church who owned a big house if she would take care of us.

The woman he asked went to the Lord and told Him she didn't want to do this. However, she wanted to know what He wanted. He asked her a question in return. "Are you believing Me for a swimming pool in your back yard?"

She said, "Yes."

He said, "If you will take this family into your home and treat them in the very best way you can, I will cause your stocks to rise so that you can sell some and pay for a swimming pool."

We arrived on a Friday as I was speaking that night and all that weekend. The first indication I had this would be an unusual stay is that she put my husband and myself in hers and her husbands own master bedroom suite. When we sat down at the dinner table, frankly, I was horrified. There were twelve dishes on the table. She had a platter of beef, a platter of chicken, a platter of fish and a platter of pork. The other eight dishes were multiple vegetables, potatoes cooked in different manners and several rice casseroles. Then for dessert there were pies, cakes, ice cream, fruit, cookies, brownies and meringues. She did her best for us.

How was I supposed to eat all that? Especially before preaching? I don't necessarily need an empty stomach, but certainly not a stuffed one. I made sure I tasted everything so I would be a good guest. My kids pigged out! They thought it was the best meal they'd ever had.

The woman wrote me a letter afterwards to explain why she had gone to such lengths for us. She told me about some stocks she owned that never moved. They stayed steady year after year. But on the Monday after we left her house, they doubled. By the next day she had sold half of them and gained enough to have a pool built in her back yard. The day after that the stocks went back to the yearly level and have never budged.

All things are possible with God. He's looking for those who actually trust Him and who are willing to obey. Part of trust and obey is to go along with His plan. Eventually we all learn that His plan is so much better than the one we can devise so why bother to instruct Him.

THE IMPORTANCE
OF OBEDIENCE

One thing slowly becomes clear as you start your walk of faith. Nothing in the spiritual realm is singular. Everything is overlapped, intertwined, connected to one another. So when the Scripture says, for example, *Here is the perseverance of the saints; here are those who keep the commandments of God and the faith of Jesus (Revelation 14:12),* you discern that the achievement of your faith requests depends on your obedience to what God tells you to do.

For instance, in those early years I got up at 5 a.m. when my husband left for work, prayed for two hours, woke the children up at 7 a.m., sent them off to school at 8 a.m. and then I read the Bible for two hours. My thirst, my passion I expressed as this, "I want to know You more!"

In the summer of 1981 I took my children for a week in Alliance Redwoods, one of the "Camps Farthest Out". As I sat in one of the meetings in this big log building with maybe 250 people present and listened to the camp Chairman give some logistical details, I heard the Lord say, "You will be up there doing that."

I whipped around to see who He was talking to. Surely not to me because being Chairman of Alliance Redwoods would have never entered my mind. You must understand at that point in my life I suffered greatly from inferiority and my natural life felt suffocated by the homosexual spirit that occupied my husband's soul. I was far too weighed down by shame, self-loathing and despondency to ever put myself in the public eye.

At the end of that week a member of the Council running the camp asked me if I would be a member of their group to plan and operate next year's camp. With awe that maybe I had heard from the Lord about being on that stage, and with trepidation because I DID NOT WANT TO BE CAMP CHAIRMAN; strictly out of obedience I accepted their invitation. But I argued with the Lord about this 'Chairman' thing.

He gave me a vision in response to my consternation. I saw myself swimming in a very deep lake. A boat floated behind me and I assumed I dove from it. Jesus swam on top of me; that's about the best way I can describe it. My head did not go beneath the water as I had my eye on the goal, but out of the corners of my eyes I could see His arms stroke through the water right beside mine and His chin seemed to rest on my head.

Answering the very thoughts in my mind He said, "You can swim in deep water," and somehow I knew I could be Chairman of the camp and that He would do it with me. That did not make me want the job. In the summer of 1982, after the camp ended the Council voted on its next Chairman. A member approached me and said there were several who wanted my name on the ballot. Would it be okay if she nominated me for Chairman?

What could I say? "No, I don't want that!" I couldn't have my will and His will too, so I said, "Okay." I won the vote, but the previous Chairman, a long time camper, claimed he would co-chair the camp with me because of my inexperience. Ah! Here was my chance. "No, thank you." I said, "Let me withdraw and you simply be Chairman again."

The Council members would have none of it. The woman who approached me said, "No to both of you. We voted on Marty, we trust her relationship with the Lord and we want her for our Chairman." They took another vote and it was unanimous. I chaired the camp for two years, and let me add that they were two years of joy!

Now let me jump ahead. One morning in my 5 a.m. prayer time, the Lord said to me, "Go to Rhema." I didn't know what that meant. I knew the word – rhema – somehow meant the Word of God, but I didn't even know it meant 'the spoken word of God'. I thought He was telling me to read the Bible more. So I read for two and one half hours each morning instead of two.

One day a friend came to visit, by this time I was well into being Chairman of the camp and she was a member of the Council. She said, "Marty, you guys ought to go to Rhema."

I said, "What's that?"

She said, "It's a Bible school in Tulsa, Oklahoma."

I wrote for applications. Mine was a breeze to fill out. My former husband had a couple of stumbling blocks. First of all they asked when he was baptized with the Holy Spirit with the initial evidence of speaking in tongues. One of their requirements. He came to me, "I don't think I have this."

"What? Of course you do. You've been baptized in the Holy Spirit for several years, just like me. You pray in tongues with the rest of us."

"I fake it."

"You fake it! Geez! Let me pray for you." I laid hands on him, asked for the baptism and immediately he began speaking in other tongues, probably those of angels.

Then he received a letter back from Rhema asking him a question. "On your application we asked when you had your last alcoholic drink and your reply was 'Last night.' What did you mean by that?" Being a non-drinker was one of their requirements.

He showed me their letter and said, "I was telling the truth. But the truth has changed. Since I wrote those flippant words, I haven't had a single alcoholic drink." This came from a man who drank two Scotch and waters after work, a half bottle of wine with dinner and usually a Cognac during the evening. But he hadn't touched a drop since finishing his application! He wanted to know what to do now. I told him to write and tell them exactly what he told me. They accepted him right away.

This all happened before the murder. Right after the murder we left for Rhema Bible School, leaving beautiful, hospitable California for nondescript, unwelcoming Oklahoma. But the school itself was heaven on earth! Four hours every day we spent taking feverish notes on the best subject in the world: the person, the life and the teachings of Jesus Christ my Lord!

One morning as I dressed for school I looked at myself in the mirror and marveled, "How did this ever happen to you?" I asked myself, "How did you ever get to this cherished and prized place of going to Bible school and not just any Bible school, but one which teaches exactly what was on your heart to learn?" I remembered my words: "I want to know You more!"

The Lord answered me as I stared into that mirror. "I couldn't have gotten you here if you hadn't accepted being

Chairman of Alliance Redwoods." That revelation exploded inside of me. I saw how obedience to do something that seems completely disconnected from the desire is essential to the accomplishment of the desire. He had to prepare me, and my husband, so that we could be ready to receive – knowing Him more.

If you are clear about what you want from the Lord, if you can substantiate that your desire is actually the desire of God by finding it in the Bible, then you can build your faith base. You can collect Scriptures that promise and confirm your request. Your next step is to focus your intention on the object, or subject, or event, or whatever you've submitted to Him to be your desire. When you focus your intention you become a vehicle for the desire. Then you must determine that you will obey God. Whatever He says you will do.

Train yourself to obey. For instance last night, because I had signed up to set tables for a community meal at church, I put everything on the tables that needed to be there. After dinner, even though I had not enlisted for clean up, I cleared the tables I set. Carrying some still full coffee cups into the kitchen I found the sink full of dish soap so I couldn't empty them. The woman washing the pots told me to take the pitchers to another sink I hadn't known about and wash them out.

Caught for a moment wondering if I should tell her I wasn't on the wash up crew, I heard a voice from inside me say, "Do it." I immediately put the cups down, took the pitchers to the other sink and washed them. When I came back for the cups they were gone. On the way home the Lord told me that woman has chronic back pain and then I remembered her telling me about it sometime before. If she was suffering she didn't need someone arguing with her about whether or not they had signed up to wash pitchers!

We all like to think we would obey God if the job were really big and important. But it's the little foxes that ruin the vine - little disobediences. Let Him know He can trust you. Just obey.

I've known people who have believed God for a fancy car. They also believed that the desire for a fancy car had absolutely nothing to do with the rest of their Christian life, so they did not practice obedience. Of course they did not receive the fancy car. Many of them have had their faith demolished and are rather angry with God as if He failed them.

He didn't fail them. He doesn't mind if any of us have a fancy car. He just doesn't want the fancy car to have us. Therefore, when we come to Him for such a 'prize', He starts working on us to eliminate greed, to develop generosity, to shape us into people who can have a fancy car because it doesn't really mean anything. In fact, He can trust us to give the fancy car away if He asks us.

The Lord told me during Bible school that He was sending us to France as missionaries. I had told Him I would go anywhere He wanted to send me, even Siberia, I didn't care; I just wanted to serve Him in His plan. When He told me France I remembered what I'd said on my previous and only visit to Paris. "If I never come back it will be too soon!" Out of obedience I took my family and moved to France. One day while walking down the block in Tours He dropped a love for the French in my heart and I've never had a problem since.

Before the move I tried to pray out every angle and to learn God's thinking on the details. One such detail was what kind of a car to purchase and where to buy it. God does have a sense of humor, sometimes, in the way He answers. During Praise and Worship in one Sunday evening service I leaned over to my husband and said, "I think the Lord just told me to buy a BMW for France."

He leaned back and said, "Pray again."

Since we only bought used cars I too thought it was a weird response from the Lord. But when I prayed again, the answer still came back, "A BMW." So I dropped by a BMW car agency in Tulsa. There was a deal going on.

If we bought a car in American cash, but picked the car up in Frankfurt, Germany, we saved a lot of money. Plus, we could keep the car in Europe for one year, fully insured, and then they would ship it to our address in the States. The appeal for doing this was that the price we would pay was much less than what we could sell the car for the following year when we sold it in the States. We would have been nuts not to do such a deal. When we tried to do it a second time, for the second year, the deal had expired, but by then a Citroen executive had become one of our best friends and he got us an excellent Citroen which we drove for years.

When we signed the contract for the purchase of the BMW my mind flooded with memories of the cars the Lord asked us to give away. I never dreamed that giving away those clunkers would open the door for me to have a BMW. I liked having that fancy car, but truthfully, the petit little eight year old Diahatsu I have in France right now pleases me just as much. God led me to this car in a similar fashion as He did to the BMW. One isn't better than the other. What counts is my walk of obedience.

> *...Has the Lord as great delight in burnt offerings and sacrifices, as in obeying the voice of the Lord? Behold, to obey is better than sacrifice... (1 Samuel 15:22).*

I cannot say enough about obedience; it is the key to any progress Christians make in Christ. What He asks you to do may sound stupid sometimes – just do it! A friend of mine, an agile man, used to collect pennies, climb up on a statue of an angel in a city park and put them in the marble hand. He also wrote a little word of encouragement on a scrap of paper and put the pennies on top of it so it wouldn't blow away. He said the Lord told him to do this and he'd been doing it for years.

An impoverished neighborhood surrounded this lovely park and lonely boys frequented the playgrounds, the fields and they especially congregated around the statue. My friend had to fill the hand early in the morning on his way to teach school so he wouldn't be caught. One afternoon he took me with him to observe.

The neighborhood kids knew about the pennies and the notes but no one commandeered the statue. As we watched the kids gathered there after school, shouting at each other, "Whose turn is it?" Finally a little guy shyly said he thought it was his turn. He had to be helped up the statue to reach into the hand and someone else had to read the note outloud. It simply said, "God is your Daddy and He loves you very much."

The kids cheered and clapped the boy on the back, "Hey, you got a good one!" and then they drifted off to play basketball or kickball or some other activity. Older boys had also come to watch and turned away afterwards without being sarcastic or ruining the little boys' pleasure. I nearly cried. Here were all these fatherless boys sharing a treasure from an angel's hand that assuaged their souls. I've lost track of my friend, but I'm sure the reward for his obedience was great.

Let me remind you of the Israelites after they left Egypt. Their stroll to Canaan land should have taken 11 days. Instead it took over 40 years. Do you remember why? They disobeyed. To fulfill His promise and their faith for a land of their own, God had to wait until all the disobedient ones died. Then He could bring the ones who believed Him, who trusted Him, who obeyed Him into the Promised Land.

For the children of Israel walked forty years in the wilderness, till all the people who were men of war, who came out of Egypt, were consumed, because they did not obey the voice of the Lord... (*Joshua 5:6*).

The Lord told Moses He was giving the land of Canaan to them. It was in that statement of fact that they should have believed. Then He instructed Moses to send spies into Canaan. They came back with a branch of the fruit to show the people how God had blessed the land. Artists have portrayed that branch as holding grapes each one the size of a man's head!

The spies gave a bad report. *Yeah, the fruit's great but you should see the giants! They'll kill us all!* So the people wailed and complained and refused to go. Caleb, however, stuck with God's report that He was giving them the land so it didn't matter if the giants were ten times taller than their already frightening height. He proclaimed they would win because God was fighting for them. He already promised the land. Caleb and Joshua, who also came back with a good report, were the only ones of that generation to enter the Promised Land.

If you're wondering right now how to determine if God is saying something, giving you a task to do, or if it's the devil trying to horn in on your life, then remember all good gifts come down from God in heaven. The task He gives you to do will either be good or will lead to goodness. Satan can try to forge goodness, but God knows your heart. If you are genuinely trying to please God your Father, then it is better to err on the side of obedience, than to err on the side of resistance or rebellion. Just do it and trust God to stop you if it's not Him.

You might ask, "Can't I just live my own life? Can't I just get born again and get into heaven without all this obedience stuff?" My answer to that is "Of course." But it is a moot question. The thing about Jesus living inside of you is that He puts an intense desire in you to please God. Why is that? I mean is God after some kind of slavery mentality here? Let me give you the simple truth: your Creator knows you better than you know yourself and His desire is that His creation has a satisfying, peaceful, creative, loving, productive life and He knows just how to get that for you. Through obedience He will form you, place you, position you for profound victory, decorous triumph, jubilant overcoming and you will know peace and prosperity, His Shalom.

Obedience can be a nuisance; obedience can be scary; obedience can be time consuming; obedience can be boring; obedience can be costly. I could continue that list forever and I think I have experienced them all. I've said this before in another book but it bears repeating. The Jews have a saying: 'I will do God's will as if it is my will so that He will do my will as if it is His will.' If you want to speed God's progress in bringing your faith to fruition – obey Him!

THE DESTRUCTION
OF DOUBT

The biggest faith battle I fought I waged against my former husband's homosexuality. I won't go into great detail here as the whole story is written up in my book *Sleeping with Demons* where I write about myself through the character Maggie Dubois. I encourage everyone to read that book as homosexuality touches all our lives.

We'd been married ten years when he told me he "liked boys." I thought I should leave him, but I really didn't want to and I'm glad I stayed. We became Christians several years after that and yes, in case you are wondering, a man can get born again and even Spirit filled without dislodging the homosexual spirit.

How can I say that? Very easy. Follow this spiritual understanding: if a man's spirit has not been filled by the homosexual spirit, if the homosexual spirit only afflicts the man's soul and body, then God has access to the man. The spirit is who we are and if a man is simply oppressed by homosexuality in his soul and body, he is not a homosexual. We are spirits, we have souls and we live in bodies. It is the spirit that gets born again and the spirit that gets filled with the Holy Spirit. Only a man whose spirit has been taken over by the homosexual spirit can call himself a homosexual and those men are hardened against God.

Look at it this way: when do we call a man a thief? If he steals something because he is hungry, do we call him a thief? If he likes to think about stealing and he spends time imagining himself stealing things he'd like to own, but he never does it, do we call him a thief? No. We call him a thief when stealing has become his lifestyle or he makes his living from stealing. In other words a thief is one who has surrendered himself to stealing. A homosexual is one who has surrendered himself to homosexuality.

I can hear some of you sputtering, "But God hates homosexuality!" I'm sure He does. He hates all things that damage man. Think about that. God, who is made of love, hates something. When you study it out in the Bible you find He never hates a human being. He created every baby ever born and He never stops loving that child, no matter how far away from Him that child wanders. He loves the man and hates homosexuality. The spirit of homosexuality is so destructive that a man afflicted by that spirit is hard to reach. God passionately wants all men set free.

Once I became a Christian, getting my husband delivered from this affliction became my mandate in life. What else do you call it, really, besides an affliction? Simply stated it is Satan afflicting people so that they won't fulfill the call God has on their lives. So I set out to put my faith to work and daily it failed.

I belonged to a large church, about 5,000 members, and we had a separate service on Thursday nights for people suffering from addictions. Their spouses also attended. About 200 people frequented this special service and afterwards we broke into small groups for sharing and discussing the sermon we had just heard. My small group consisted of wives of men tormented by sexual deviation.

Every Thursday I listened to these women share how they stood in faith for their husband's deliverance. Some of the women kept falling, pretty much like I did. They didn't come to the group too often and usually dropped out. But the vast majority of them reported increasing victories until their husbands were indeed set free. I latched on to what these victorious women had to say and did my best to apply their techniques. I didn't drop out. In fact they asked me to lead the group, in spite of my defeats.

Every day I spoke out words of freedom, something like this: "In the name of Jesus Christ of Nazareth I command the spirit of homosexuality to leave my husband and never return. I apply the Blood of Jesus to his body and soul to cleanse him, forgive him and protect him. I claim that no weapon formed against him will ever prosper for he is the righteousness of God through Christ. Amen!"

Those words should have worked, shouldn't they? The Bible says that faith comes by hearing and hearing by the Word of God. The Bible instructs us to speak our faith.

And since we have the same spirit of faith, according to what is written, "I believed and therefore I spoke," we also believe and therefore speak (2 Corinthians 4:13).

I said those words so I could hear them and they contained the Word of God. I just didn't account for two tiny little problems.

Well, maybe not so tiny, in fact these problems are so big they are the major stumbling blocks in the Christian life! But they appear to be so miniscule and helpless that one forgets their power until long after the battle is lost. The first one is doubt and unbelief.

But let him ask in faith, with no doubting, for he who doubts is like a wave of the sea driven and tossed by the wind (James 1:6).

You can remember from the Bible that Jesus went to preach in his hometown of Nazareth when his reputation was enormous. Everyone heard of his great healings and his powerful preaching which brought on signs and wonders. Yet in his own hometown it says he could do no mighty works. Why not? Because the people were filled with unbelief. They knew this kid Jesus. He'd grown up there. Who did He think He was blowing into town like a big shot? He was just the carpenter's boy.

Like those townspeople I knew my former husband. I knew how mean he could be. I confess; I doubted. I'd start out fine every day. Then something would happen, usually something he said to belittle me. He complained about everything, but really, it wasn't exactly everything, it was just everything about me. For example, unless we had company my former husband sat at the dinner table and looking at the food I served would say something like, "Well, what kind of road kill are we having tonight?" Since being a woman hater kind of rides along with homosexuality, I'd take his comments rather personally and my hopes would fade.

The next day I'd start over because doubt kills faith. If there is one enemy we have to grab by the nape of the neck, shake it until it pays attention and then tell it to get out of our lives, its doubt. Doubt will ruin everything.

Peter is an example of this. In the middle of a big storm the disciples were in a boat on the Sea of Galilee when Jesus came walking by on the water. Peter yelled at him over the wind and the waves, *"Lord, if that's You…."* This always makes me laugh. Who else would it be? Jesus was there in the flesh, not like seeing some ghost, which they quickly determined it was not, so who could have said, 'No, Peter. It's Barack Obama.' Or some other name. Nobody else walked on water in the flesh.

Then it makes me realize Peter had Jesus cornered because his full sentence was, *"Lord, if that is You, command me to come to You on the water" (Matthew 14:28).* What could Jesus possibly say? 'No, Peter, it's not Me. So don't come.'

However, He does say *"Come"* and Peter gets out of the boat, full of faith, knowing he can do it because he has the Word of God on it, he's heard it with his own ears. He knows it's possible because with his own eyes he's watching Jesus do it. Peter walks on the water! Victory! We all know what happened next. Peter looked at the wind and the waves. He stopped watching Jesus. Doubt filled his soul and he started to sink. Doubt ruined everything.

When we fall, however, God holds us up with His hand. That's what Jesus did. He reached out His hand and lifted Peter up. That's what happened to me every evening, every morning. I'd go to bed in doubt and wake up to the hand of the Lord lifting me up and I'd start over.

With hindsight I can look back and see what a tremendous burden my doubt and unbelief were to my former husband. It was like throwing buckets of defeat on him. Are we excused from having faith because our feelings have been hurt? Read 1 Corinthians 13 and tell me what you think. What a mess I was to the cause. God had to get me out of the way.

What is faith for anyway? Jesus makes it very clear and He is not speaking figuratively: *Have the faith of God. For assuredly, I say to you, whoever says to this mountain, 'Be removed and be cast into the sea,' and does not doubt in his heart, but believes that those things he says will be done, he will have whatever he says (Mark 11:22-23).*

Faith is for moving mountains. Those mountains can be any size; whatever is blocking your life is a mountain. My former husband's homosexuality was a mountain and my faith could have removed it, but everyday I folded. I had the evidence before my eyes of seeing those happy, victorious couples in our Addicts Service and I chose to look at the wounding words and hurtful circumstances, just like Peter's wind and waves.

The second tiny little problem which defeats faith, because it is actually a monumental stumbling block, is that of not being in agreement. It never occurred to me that lack of agreement could be a problem until I threatened my former husband with divorce. Suddenly his life seemed to turn around. I'd walk into the living room and there he'd be on his knees praying. I'd quietly retreat so as not to disturb him by my heart pounding wildly in my chest in the hope that I would really have the husband I longed for, a partner in my spiritual life! Yea! Hallelujah!

I'd find him turning on praise and worship music and lifting his hands to heaven as if in a glorious state of ecstasy over his love for my Lord Jesus. At first these things impressed me considerably, but after about two weeks

I felt something was wrong so I asked the Lord about it. He caused me to realize that my husband was not sharing his encounters with me. He was right! Why not? Anyone I know who has experiences with Jesus on a personal, intimate level wants to share those moments because they are so wonderful.

After one of his praise and worship sessions I asked my husband what he had seen or experienced in the Holy Spirit. He looked at me quizzically and didn't answer.

I tried to help him, 'You know, what did it feel like?"

"What's it supposed to feel like?"

"It's different for everybody."

Then he became defensive, "It didn't feel like anything to me."

After several attempts I realized he wasn't going to share so I quit. He did, too.   All his spiritual pretense left.   No more prayer time; no more praise and worship. The Lord, gracious teacher that He is, explained to me that my husband was not in agreement with me.   He didn't want to change. He didn't want to be free and so he wouldn't be.   People have to be in agreement in order to accomplish something. I couldn't force my faith on him. He was happy with the way things were. He would make a pretense in order to keep me from divorcing him, but he couldn't keep it up. Pretending is always a strain.

The best thing I ever did for my husband was to divorce him. Separating from him stripped away my doubt and unbelief which, spiritually and soulishly speaking, were heavy burdens on him. I can look back and see how my doubt and unbelief acted like concrete boots on his feet! All his supports were pulled out from underneath him and without those concrete boots he was on shaky ground. He didn't know how to act. Yes, he felt abandoned because he had followed me and expected me to take care of him forever.

Therefore, the divorce made him take responsibility for the presence of homosexuality in his life. He had to decide; what did he want to do? Thank God he decided he wanted to be free. It was no longer Marty wanting him to be free, it was him wanting something for his own life and with that he could step into faith before God. He discovered he wasn't abandoned because Jesus never left him and He never would. He learned the best supports are the everlasting arms of God who carry him through every difficulty right into victory.

It took three years living in a Christian center built to help men come out of sexual deviation for my former husband to fully and totally kick the spirit of homosexuality out of his life. We have remained very good friends. Every few months or so, during those three years, I asked him if he were free and he would honestly say no. Then it got to be he'd have to think about it before he could give me an answer and finally he said, "I don't know where it went, but one morning I woke up and I knew it was gone."

At his 'graduation', the moment of celebration in the center where they bless the man as he enters the new life he has achieved, his director told the crowd he had never seen a harder heart toward God than what my former husband had. But he had also never seen anyone work harder to be free than my former husband had. At one point he read the Word four hours a day and prayed four hours a day. I'm very proud of him. He's now on staff at that Center helping men who come from all over the world to conquer those homosexual spirits, kick them out and open up their souls and bodies for the habitation of the Holy Spirit.

If there is one hurdle to master in life it is the destructive voice of doubt. Take control of doubt and you will go from faith to faith, or we could say, take control of doubt and you will go from victory to victory. Choose to believe. Confirm your beliefs with the Word of God. Only the Truth is worthy of your belief and only the Word of God is the Truth. Associate with people with whom you are in agreement. Lack of agreement will bring all progress to a complete halt, while agreement will swiftly set your cause running to fulfillment.

The end of the story is that my faith did work. My former husband is free.

THE PART OF THE STORY
NO ONE WANTS TO HEAR

Remember my million dollars? This is the side of the story no one wants to hear. There is something about the human spirit that allows God to bless us and then we say to Him, "Okay, God, I can take it from here," and we decide what to do next. I remember rushing to answer the front door one day during Bible School and realizing in my race for the door that I had not asked God what to do about the money now that we had most of what we were going to receive.

Instantly the response came, "Let your husband handle it while you concentrate on your studies." It was fortunate to have that response as the man at the door was a Financial Advisor hired by my husband to invest our money. He and my husband sat me down and he told me, "You are not to spend one dime of this money. Even if you want a piece of gum you must ask your husband before you buy it."

This, of course, came way before the days when I divorced my husband and he went off to live in the Assembly of God community for men with sexual deviations. So I wondered what my husband had said about me to this Financial Advisor, but I really didn't want to know. With gritted teeth I agreed to their macabre plan.

After Bible School we took off for the mission field and were amazed that occasion after occasion came up where we had to spend more money than we thought. The first Pastor we worked for asked us to go to language school before getting involved in ministry. Good idea. For one summer we worked hard at learning French, but the housing turned out to be difficult. In twelve weeks we moved eight times. It was a very expensive summer.

Then we were invited to join a national committee to produce Christian television. Long hours were spent driving back and forth to Paris with hotel bills, restaurant meals, and of course, hefty financial participation in the production. The work of the committee failed and everyone lost their money.

Our two children, who came with us on the field, had graduated from Oral Roberts University and Victory Christian School. After a year they wanted to go back home. So we had tuition to pay again, housing for them, air flights etc. All of that really wasn't too bad; what hurt the most was the fact that the Financial Advisor lost one half of our money. He invested in stocks that began an immediate slide to the bottom.

The year after our kids went back to the States we also returned. We came back because we were burned out. I had been leaving money matters in my former husband's hands; like that voice said when I rushed to the door. But when I found myself in a California motel with no house rental in sight, my furniture in route from Oklahoma and more and more motel bills and restaurant bills looming before me, I stepped in.

One morning I told my former husband he must stay in the motel as the Lord and I were going house hunting. We were in the Foothills of California, the Gold Country, and I took off driving, concentrating more on talking to Jesus than on where I was going.

The first question I asked was, "What the heck went wrong?" It had taken me three years to believe the money in and it had taken three years to lose half. How did that happen?

The Lord very quietly said, "You didn't ask me what to do with the money."

I responded heatedly, "You told me to let my husband handle the money." I suddenly knew inside of myself that a million dollars means nothing to the Lord. He is a gazillionaire. What does mean something to Him is the perfecting of His saints. Yes, He does perfect us and it takes time because it is a process. I may have grown in the acquiring of the money, learning about tithing, offerings and especially obedience to do what He says, but my husband didn't.

He seemed to go along with me. At least in most things. The Lord asked me to analyze what had happened in the last three years in regards to spending money. In doing so I realized that we had passed through a critical moment in time. The enormity of our disobedience nearly caused me to crash the car.

A certain French Evangelist had organized a large tent meeting for a week of camping. About 3,000 people were expected to attend. In my prayer time I heard the Lord ask me to film the event and make videos for sale throughout the French speaking world. My husband said yes.

We engaged an excellent film crew from Switzerland, the Evangelist agreed that we would be the official film team and we would have all rights to the end product. About five days before the event my husband panicked at the expense and cancelled everything. The owner of the film company scrambled to withdraw his contracts with his crew. The Evangelist ended up having one guy with one home movie camera film from one position and the results were totally amateurish. As I considered all the events of those two years, this was definitely the turning point toward our crash.

In that car, whirling through the Foothills, coming to grips with our state of affairs, the Lord said, "In the beginning you didn't ask Me what to do with the money." Again, that seemed unfair to me since He told me to let my husband handle the finances. But I didn't feel like bickering anymore; I simply wanted to know the truth from His point of view.

I asked the Lord, "What did You want us to do with the money from the beginning?" He told me of an apartment building in Roseville, California that He wanted us to buy for which our million dollars would have been an acceptable down payment. Had we made that purchase the building would have supplied us with more than enough money for the rest of our lives on the mission field, doing whatever the Lord asked of us.

I wondered if we could still do it with the money we had left. He said yes we could, the building had never sold, but it would be more difficult as the mortgage would have to be bigger. Eventually it would even out, but for years we would have to pay for our disobedience by living stringently. Today that apartment building is prime property and incredibly valuable, but back then today's value could only be seen through the eyes of God.

That evening I asked my husband if he would be willing to obey God now, though when I asked him I couched the words in softer terms. I asked if we could buy that building. He said, "No way! I've worked all my life and real estate is work. I'm not working another day." Sadly, I wondered how God would work this out for me.

I continued driving around the Foothills, looking, and the Lord directed me to a fabulous place to live. We stayed there for two years without either my husband or I working. During this time a friend introduced us to another Financial Advisor who wanted to invest the rest of our money into some undeveloped real estate in Oregon.

My husband figured that God wanted us to buy that apartment building, so it would probably be alright if we invested in raw land. To his mind, real estate was real estate. That's not the way God works. God is always specific. He always has the exact answer. But my husband wasn't interested in my opinion. He gave every single penny that we still owned to this Advisor who invested it in the land.

For the first time in history a certain river overflowed and flooded the undeveloped land. It stayed flooded for three years. This particular phenomenon was written up in newspapers all over the world because of the previous expected value of the land and the obvious total decline of its value with the occurrence of the flood. In other words, the Financial Advisor followed a very educated guess which should have succeeded. Except that God wasn't willing for us to succeed in our disobedience.

We lost absolutely every penny we owned and I asked the Lord why I had to suffer along with my husband. I hadn't made those terrible decisions. He did. Why punish me as well? That may sound like a selfish question and I knew it was, but I wanted an answer anyway.

The Lord said, "Because you are connected to him." I thought it funny He didn't say I was married to him, but 'connected' to him. Suddenly I realized that those with whom my soul had attached itself had a certain authority in my life. My soul was absolutely hooked to my husband's. His life had become more important than my own. Not only did he flow with my decisions, I flowed with his; and therefore whatever punishment he deserved, I deserved it too.

Several years later we divorced and five weeks after the divorce I was back in France to live and work for the Lord without any money whatsoever. That first winter was exceptionally cold and I could not afford heat. Realizing I had to start over I pulled out my Scriptures about prosperity and settled down to establish a goal. No longer content with millionaire status, I decided to go for a much larger stake. I used to tell people I was believing God for five million dollars, but that was a lie so I quit that. I'm believing for much more.

I'm not going to tell you what I've pinned my faith on, but I will tell you when it arrives. It should be soon. The Lord and I have BIG plans. One thing I realized is that God has to have something to work with when He is providing. When I believed Him for one million dollars and then when it arrived, I calculated just how much the Lord asked me to give during my waiting period. I'm talking about special giving. It was a little over $10,000. That's one percent of a million.

> ... *"Assuredly, I say to you, there is no one who has left house or brothers or sisters or father or mother or wife or children or lands, for My sake and the gospel's, 30 who shall not receive a hundredfold now in this time—houses and brothers and sisters and mothers and children and lands, with persecutions—and in the age to come, eternal life (Mark 10:29-30).*

Fields refer to livelihood, or in our day and age, money. One million dollars is a hundredfold return on ten thousand. I've had to give away a lot more to have it be one percent of what I am believing for now and if my calculations are correct, I'm just about there.

I hope I'm not making this into a cold and calculating tale. It's not. It's a joy to give, like I said earlier. I try only to give where God tells me to. I say 'try' because sometimes my own compassion gets in the way and sometimes my own defiance keeps me from giving where I should. These, of course, are setbacks to my goal.

God is a giver. He wants us to want to be just like Him, so He sets the guidelines to help us along the way. I'm within the parameters of those guidelines and my faith is strong. I will receive. In the meantime I am no longer without heat! God has met every need and increased my ability to live and to give as time passes. He's a good God, a good provider. I love him with all my heart and soul!

GROWING FAITH

I like Jesus' question that He asked when He was preaching on a hillside by the Sea of Galilee. We call that sermon The Beatitudes. *Now if God so clothes the grass of the field, which today is, and tomorrow is thrown into the oven, will He not much more clothe you, O you of little faith? (Matthew 6:30).*

When God created grass He said it was **"Good."** His creation satisfied Him. When He created you He said you were **"Very good."** You more than satisfied Him; you brought Him joy. He is going to take care of you because He is delighted with you. You may not be delighted with you, but that's another story. Furthermore, you might as well be satisfied with you, the Creator of the Universe is! In other words, stop talking yourself out of your faith walk because you don't believe you are worthy or that you deserve it. That's not for you to decide.

When Jesus fell asleep in the boat and a white squall tore into the sea, savagely battering the little ship, the disciples woke Him up. He said to the sea, ***"Peace, be still."*** The sea instantly became flat and calm. They were stupefied.

> ***But He said to them, "Why are you so fearful? How is it that you have no faith?" (Mark 4:40).***

I think if I had been a disciple in that boat I might have thought, 'Faith? Who knew we could speak to a raging sea and it would obey us? Who knew we could have faith like that?' Of course we have the benefit of time distance and hearing this story since our early childhood. But perhaps that's not a benefit because I don't see many Christians speaking to the elements.

We lived in Tours, France for two years and I taught Bible studies in Chatellerault and in Le Mans. Driving home at night from Chatellerault, especially, was so dangerous because of the heavy ground fog. Usually I would have to drive with my head out the window to follow the center line in the highway, otherwise I couldn't see.

I got tired of this so I took authority over the fog. I told it to lift off and never bother me again in the name of Jesus and it obeyed. What happened to the fog on nights when I wasn't driving that road, I don't know. But then I don't care. I wanted it out of my way and so I commanded it.

When my son graduated from Bible school in Oklahoma, a classmate invited us all to her house for a graduation party. One of the guests came running in the house shouting about a tornado coming our way. We rushed into the back yard and sure enough it was a few houses away coming right at us, spraying boards from houses it chewed up in its path. We shouted at it to lift off the ground and not touch us or the property we were in or our cars on the street out front. Then we watched as it did just that. It lumbered overhead and dropped down on the other side of the house and continued on its destructive path.

> *First, I thank my God through Jesus Christ for you all, that your faith is spoken of throughout the whole world" (Romans 1:8).*

Paul, in his letter to the Romans, is telling them he thanks God for them. Why? Because their faith is famous! Wouldn't you love to have people know you by your faith? Can't you see them pointing their fingers at you exclaiming over how pleasing you are to God and how much you've accomplished for His Kingdom by exercising your faith? It's possible. Faith belongs to you. What are you going to do with it? Move mountains, I hope! Help people, I hope!

In that same letter Paul speaks about Abraham and uses his faith as an example to teach the Romans how to exercise their faith. *And not being weak in faith, he did not consider his own body, already dead (since he was about a hundred years old), and the deadness of Sarah's womb. He did not waver at the promise of God through unbelief, but was strengthened in faith, giving glory to God, (Romans 4:19-20).*

In spite of all contrary circumstances, Abraham strengthened his faith. He trusted God to do what He said He would do. Somehow I imagine Abraham out there in the desert, maybe playing a lute or having one played and singing about the glory of God. When the focus is on God it's easy to believe for the impossible. He can do anything!

> **God is faithful, by whom you were called into the fellowship of His Son, Jesus Christ our Lord (1 Corinthians 1:9).**

He's the only trustworthy One! If He wants you to believe Him in order to change your circumstances, then by all means, DO IT! Believe Him for changes in your life. Kick doubt out! Simply trust the only trustworthy One. Sing about it. That's what David did. Sing out your gratitude before you have anything to be grateful about. Before you see any fruit from your faith, thank God that He has already given and you have already received because you know it's on the way!

> **And though I have the gift of prophecy, and understand all mysteries and all knowledge, and though I have all faith, so that I could remove mountains, but have not love, I am nothing (1 Corinthians 13:2).**

Remember that once you put your faith in motion, God is going to prepare your whole being to be ready to receive. Whatever you are lacking, He's going to work on that. Be obedient. Observe His testing and conform yourself to His ideal.

> **But that no one is justified by the law in the sight of God is evident, for "the just shall live by faith" (Galatians 3:11).**

Faith is not just a here and there thing. Faith, trusting God for all and in all things, is a minute by minute procedure. Faith is now your life. Live it fully.

> **Above all, taking the shield of faith with which you will be able to quench all the fiery darts of the wicked one (Ephesians 6:16).**

Nobody wants the devil messing with their lives. How do you get him to stay away? Hang some garlic around your neck? Say a mantra? No, nothing foolish like that. You live so steadily in faith that it becomes a permanent shield around you and that faith shield extinguishes the fiery arrows the devil throws at you. Your faith shield ruins Satan's plans.

> **Hold fast the pattern of sound words which you have heard from me, in faith and love which are in Christ Jesus (2 Timothy 1:13).**

Only say what you want to have happen. Don't talk about evil. If someone talks to you about the bad things that could happen, turn it around in your response. Remember a believer receives what a believer believes. You will speak what you believe. Make sure you believe what you want to receive so that you only speak positive words that reinforce what you will receive.

You've been given a great gift, a servant named Faith. It is up to you to determine what you are going to do with it. In this book I've tried to be very open with my life to demonstrate some failures and some successes; and I hope my examples have helped you. I encourage you to build your faith; make it grow. It's the greatest gift you can give God. It's what pleases Him. And as you grow I pray you may be able to say with Paul:

> *I have been crucified with Christ; it is no longer I who live, but Christ lives in me; and the life which I now live in the flesh I live by faith in the Son of God, who loved me and gave Himself for me (Galatians 2:20).*

MY CONFESSIONS

Through His Word God reveals Himself as our Rock, our Husband, our Strength, our Shield, our Refuge, our Help, just to name a few of His attributes. He reveals His name as El Shaddai, the God who is more than enough! (Genesis 17:1) Jehovah Jireh, the God who provides for you. (Genesis 22:14) Jehovah Rapha, the God who heals you. (Exodus 15:26) Jehovah Nissi, the God who is your banner of victory over you. (Exodus 17:15) Jehovah Shalom, the God who gives you peace. (Judges 6:24) Jehovah Rohi, the God who is our shepherd. (Psalm 23:1) Jehovah Tsidkenu, the God who is our righteousness. (Jeremiah 23:6) Just to name a few of His names. There is nothing we could ever need that God cannot supply. He has just one requirement for obtaining His help in every domain: FAITH.

How do we get that faith? Through the infusion of His Word. The Word is to the soul what food is to the body. If we can get our protective, defensive, suspicious souls to actually believe the Word and expect it to happen in our lives, God will do what He says. So we have to build up our faith. If we will say something to ourselves often enough, we will believe it, good or bad.

The way we build our faith in God is by hearing the Word over and over. Who is going to say the Word to us over and over? We are. We're going to take the Word and chew on it like a bone by muttering it, contemplating it, imagining it and planting it firmly in us. When we believe what we say, we will have it. Power is in the Word.

Jesus said the flesh profits nothing. He said it is His Word that gives life. He said the Word is truth. God said that without faith it is impossible to please Him and that faith comes by hearing the Word of God. So put the Word in you and have the best of the best in this life as well as the life to follow.

We are the loves of God's life. We are everything to Him. He wants to do for us all that His Word says. But consider this: how much time do you like to spend with someone whose opinion is always the opposite of yours? It gets pretty tiring after awhile, doesn't it? God does not want to spend time with you worrying, or doubting. He doesn't worry and He doesn't doubt.

Don't you want your loved ones to choose to love you and to choose to be in agreement with you? That's what God wants. So please Him by choosing to love Him and choosing to be in agreement with Him throwing away all worry and doubt. That stuff comes from the devil anyway.

He wants you to come to Him in faith. Come to Him in gratitude, not complaining, not whining, but thankful for what His Word says because when you believe it, it will soon come to pass!

The following are some general confessions you can make over your life and support them with the Scriptures.

Thank God for these words that He has put in His guidebook, the Bible, and fellowship with Him over His promises. He wrote them for you! He made those promises just for you! Believe them and receive them!

1. I have the mind of Christ! (1 Cor 2:16)
2. I know all things! (1 Jn 2:20)
3. The anointing teaches me! (1 Jn 2:27)
4. I am anointed with the Spirit of God! (2 Cor 1:21-22)
5. I know all the truth and I know things to come! (Jn 16:13-15)
6. The Holy Spirit causes me to remember everything Jesus said! (Jn 14:26)
7. I am quick to repent, to open my mind to God and to overcome old thoughts! (Rev 3:19-21)
8. I believe Jesus Christ paid for my death, sickness and poverty which I deserved because of sin! (Mk 1:15)
9. I renew my mind daily in the Word of God! (Rom 12:2)
10. The spirit of my mind is renewed! (Eph 4:23)
11. I no longer fulfill the lusts of my mind! (Eph 2:1-3)
12. I bring every thought captive to Jesus. If that thought did not come from Him I throw it away! (2 Cor 10:4-5)
13. Everything I do prospers because I meditate in the Word! (Ps 1:1-3)
14. I think about things that are true, noble, just, pure, lovely, of good report, of virtue and that are praiseworthy! (Php 4:8)

ABOUT THE AUTHOR

Marty Delmon comes from a long line of believers. Imprisoned in England for their beliefs, her family came to the New World as Quakers. The other branch came as Methodists. Her great-grandfather, an itinerate minister, wrote in his journal, "The women of my family will publish the Good News of Jesus Christ." Marty is the first to fulfill that prophetic word.

Born in Kansas City, Missouri she claims Minnesota as her state since that's where she spent her high school years. That's also where she developed her love for sports: tobogganing, ice skating, skiing, and swimming. She swam briefly in the Aqua Follies, deterred only by a belligerent toe which cramped the minute it hit the river.

Attending school at Lindenwood College for Women in St. Charles, Missouri, Marty majored in Physical Education and thereafter taught school in San Francisco, California. She married John Pierre Delmon and they produced first a boy, Jeffrey John and then a girl, Jolie Pier.

When the children were ages 7 and 4, Marty's husband confessed his homosexuality. This admission began a long trial of psychologists, counselors, ministers and others who tried to help John overcome his 'condition.' In that epoch everyone believed homosexuals were born that way and there was no help, however, John and Marty plowed on.

During this time of great depression on her part, Jesus surprised Marty by showing up in her life and she became born again.   She and her husband attended Rhema Bible Training Center and taking the children, now 18 and 21, they moved to France as missionaries, lasting only three years.

The best thing she did for her husband was to divorce him which made him take responsibility for his 'condition.' He moved into a Christian facility which helps men overcome their sexual deviations.   Hence Marty wrote her first book, *Sleeping With Demons*, detailing their path and his subsequent deliverance.

Five weeks after the divorce Marty returned to France as a single missionary.   She settled in La Garde Freinet and established a radio ministry where her stories are heard on 107 Francophone stations.   She also pioneered a church and taught in a Bible school.   Joining International Pentecostal Holiness Church, she returned to the States for three years to raise funds.   Back in France she moved to Baillargues outside of Montpellier and focused all her energies on writing.   She discontinued public ministry except in the States where she went yearly to raise money.

Out of this intense period of writing, Marty produced 14 books, several stage plays and hundreds of stories for the radio.   Her second book, and to date the most successful, is entitled *Buried Lies*, a novel.   In her early days of Christianity, in order to lift her out of internal chaos, the Lord gave her a prayer process which plucks the lie out of the soul and plants God's truth instead. As she became freer the Lord asked her to write about the process.

When people read *Buried Lies* they asked Marty to lead workshops. Then they asked her to write a workbook so they could do the process at home. Thus, *Buried Lies Companion Workbook* came into being. Marty also recorded it as an audio book.

Her next novel came out of a certain romance from her youth and is called *Wild Card*. Now she awaits the launching of her current novel *Wild Fire*, a book about The Last Great Revival.

She also has written very effective books describing and explaining the powerful themes in the Bible. She calls them the "Destined" series: *Destined for Healing, Destined for Success, Destined for Love, Destined for Faith, Destined for Grace, Destined for Joy, Destined to Live in the Kingdom.* With more to come.

Marty has recently moved to Neauphle Le Chateau outside of Paris to be closer to her radio studio and the publication of her books. Her son Jeff, his wife Vicky and their two children Alex and Natasha live in Washington, D.C. Her daughter Jolie and her three girls Brittany, Victoria and Madison live in Tulsa, Oklahoma.

A Message from the Author

You are perfect you. No one can be more perfectly you than you are. God made you completely unique so there can be no duplicate, no substitute. He made you for Himself and He knows you because there is nobody else like you.

Yes, you have two natures. When the sperm from your father joined the egg from your mother, one nature came into being which governs your body and your soul. This nature is a fallen one, inherited from all your generations back to the original sin.

When that sperm and egg became one, more was created than a stem cell. At conception God breathed into you your spirit which is your divine nature, a portion of the Spirit of God. God is Love and God is Light. Your spirit is made of love and light.

About the age of twelve a certain portion of your brain began its appointed time of development: the ability to reason and make decisions on your own. You, like everyone else, learned you could choose between good and evil – not just be naughty or nice – but to choose evil and you found you could, at least for awhile, live with its consequences. Or you could choose good and receive its gracious and glorious rewards.

Unfortunately, choosing evil overrode your conscience, the gateway to your spirit. You seared your conscience and the door between the fallen nature and the divine nature stood open like a rusty gate. Sadly, your divine nature became corrupt like your fallen nature.

You can't just clean up a corrupt spirit; you have to exchange it for a new one. How is that possible? God already gave you your portion of His Spirit. So how do you get another one? You accept the gift of Jesus Christ. He came to take your place, to pay for what you did wrong, to erase your sins and give you a portion of His Spirit.

He blew on His disciples, they received His Spirit and became born again. He continues to breathe on new believers today. Whenever anyone says, "Jesus, I have sinned against You, Your Father and the Kingdom of God..." (see the rest of this prayer at the end of this discourse) and sincerely means it, Jesus will give him or her a new spirit.

You can be born again. Once you have received your new birth you can get your soul saved and your body will follow suit because your body does whatever your soul tells it to do. How do you get your soul saved? Obeying the Spirit of God with a willing heart one step at a time cleans up your soul and works your salvation from the inside, where your spirit man is, through the soul, your mind, emotions and will, to the outside to be expressed in your body.

Only those who receive Jesus as Lord today will live tomorrow in the Kingdom of God forever. Those who do not receive Him as their Lord will spend eternity in the kingdom of darkness. Choose today. Start your Eternal Life by giving yourself to Jesus and making Him your Lord. Love and Light will once again reside in your new spirit and He will give you His abundant life.

THE SINNER'S PRAYER

Jesus, I have sinned against You, Your Father and the Kingdom of God. I've made a mess of things by trying to run my own life and running away from you. Please forgive me. Please apply the blood You so painfully shed to pay for my sins to my spirit, soul and body. I receive You now, Jesus, as my Savior, my Lord, my best Friend, my Master and my Commander in Chief. I will love You, I will serve You, I will honor You, I will proclaim You all the days of my life and I will live with You for eternity in Heaven, the Kingdom of Love. Thank You, Jesus! I am Yours! Amen.

MORE BOOKS
by Marty Delmon

SLEEPING WITH DEMONS
www.tatepublishing.com

Married to a man caught in the trap of sexual deviation, Maggie Dubois takes us on her lone journey through the dark valleys of one-sided marriage. Her passage through the somber alley of longing for love is a story that applies to us all.

Denying the existence of the problem, homosexuality, Maggie is ensnared in the conflict. The climax of the book comes when Maggie breaks through the veil of confusion to recognize the truth and confront the spiritual darkness. Exorcising the evil from her life, Maggie walks free.

"Lessons of Life" could well be a subtitle of this book as Maggie guilelessly shares her insights and revelations of what she discovers as she feels her way through the morass. Her discoveries liberate not only herself but her husband as well. Maggie's victory is everyone's victory: truth and freedom.

BURIED LIES
www.tatepublishing.com

No action evokes as much violent emotion and reaction as does incest. Murder, suicide, hatred, imprisonment, all things ugly in life evolve from this insidious trap set in a female child by her father. Journey with seven women as they confront their past, unearth the lies they have believed about themselves, replacing them with the truth and see the changes made in their lives today. Against all odds, these seven overcame the most heinous of sins: sex forced upon them by Daddy.

Between the ages of 8 and 17 my stepfather perfunctorily raped me. At age 17, I confided in a girl friend and she encouraged me to confront him, asking why he would do such a thing. It never occurred to me I had the personal power to get him to stop, but when I followed her advice, he quit. The trauma stayed with me, however, coloring my future and damaging my potential until I received Jesus as my Lord.

The Holy Spirit led me into a prayer process in which Jesus helped me to uncover the lies I believed about myself because of what happened to me. The important part was that He planted the truth in me to replace those lies. It has made all the difference in my life.

Through the course of interviewing people for the stories I write for radio, I discovered that almost one woman out of two suffered what I suffered in my childhood. I have helped some to unearth the lies and believe the truth, but a book about it will reach far more women than I personally can reach. Therefore I have written Buried Lies.

BURIED LIES
COMPANION WORKBOOK

 When I came to the Lord I carried a lot of baggage. My illegitimate birth, the continual raping by my stepfather between the ages of 8 and 17, my mother telling me I was too stupid to be a writer so I abandoned my passion, the self-sabotage I committed when I broke up with the love of my life because he was 'too good for me', and then the man I did marry, after ten years of marriage and two children, confessed he was gay.

The Lord gave me a prayer process to clear out the chaos in my life which came not because of all these things that happened to me, but because of the lies I believed about myself because of what happened. I called that book Buried Lies. When people read Buried Lies they asked me to do a workshop to lead them through the prayer process. I thought this to be good as it took me seven hours to complete my first process simply because the prayer is intensely focused and I wasn't accustomed to praying that thoroughly.

Then they asked for a workbook to take home so that they could continue to pull out lies and plant the truth. I decided to put the whole workshop into the workbook, leaving space at the end for them to go through the process themselves and journal about it.

My publisher came up with the best idea when he put the workbook on CD. He even allowed me to do the recording. Now people can take the workshop anywhere they want and the final of the four CDs leads the listener through the prayer process. There is one more prayer to go through which the Lord also gave me for the purpose of hearing Him more clearly. I call it 'The Garden'.

WILD CARD
www.tatepublishing.com

His dream…. Ron La Fave had charted his path and meticulously pursued it. Deflecting every distraction and breaking his own heart in the process, he persevered to the point of wounding his loved ones as he doggedly attained the success that powered his dreams.

But, Ron failed to recognize the reality of evil. Dreams can be sabotaged from within, yet the threat from without comes like a sidewinder. One strike, one puncture and the aspiration deflates like a party balloon flailing wildly about the room.

Wherever he turned, the serpent hoisted its evil head. His Board of Directors threw him out; his wife left; his mentor disowned him; his bank accounts closed; his reputation tanked and the industry blackballed him. Left with nothing, he retreated to Jackson Hole.

Counting on the mountains to restore him, he hid in the Tetons. However, a certain Presence wouldn't leave. Ron found himself grappling with distractions he could not deflect and instead of the peace he sought, he tormentedly confronted good and evil.

Learning to accept the one and reject the other, a spiritual path opened which revealed success beyond his wildest dreams. Suddenly, every conflict in life resolved itself.

DESTINED FOR SUCCESS
www.rpjandco.com

Isaiah foretold the cross, the price Jesus would pay and the benefits we would receive. He mentioned prosperity. "The chastisement of our prosperity was upon Him," Is 53:5. The Hebrew word is SHALOM! While the translators used the word 'peace' in this verse, both prosperity and peace are the meanings of SHALOM. The two words are interchangeable. Can you have peace without prosperity? Doesn't prosperity bring peace? Jesus paid for you to have prosperity. It's a new-birth right. **Destined for Success** defines that prosperity and directs you to the path to receive it. SHALOM!

DESTINED FOR HEALING
www.rpjandco.com

All around the author sees unnecessary sickness and pain. She sees people trying to explain away their failure at being healed. The author knows from personal experience the triumph of overcoming the disease of the body and wanted to share the knowledge she's gained. May the Body of Christ truly be transformed by accepting the healing that Jesus bought for us with His body.

DESTINED FOR LOVE
www.rpjandco.com

Love is a force. Without a doubt it is the strongest force on the earth. For example, faith works by love and we know that we cannot please God without faith, hence, without love there can be no faith and without faith there is no pleasing God. In **Destined for Love**, Author Marty Delmon takes us on a journey through the

Bible to demonstrate what love is, how to use it and what amazing results are intrinsically woven into the practice of love.

Jesus gave the Body of Christ one command: those who live in the Kingdom of God would be known by those who do not as Christians. How would the unsaved know that certain ones are Christians? By our love for others living in the Kingdom. Not by our love for the world. The world abuses the gifts given to them, but when they see how much we Christians love each other a certain hunger is created. How much love for one another do we actually see in our churches? Are we making the unsaved jealous yet?

Christians are DESTINED FOR LOVE. The question is, will we fulfill our destiny? Will we find the source of all good things coming down from the Father of Lights? It is essential to understand love because the promises of God are all based on love. In all honesty we have to answer the question that asks if we have been having trouble receiving what we need and want from God. Maybe the answer can be found in how much love we are giving.

About the Publisher

In 2004, the Spirit of God birthed RPJ & Company according to Romans 14:17.

RPJ & Company, Inc. began publishing Christian books for pastors, leaders, ministers, missionaries, and others with a message to help the Body of Christ. Our published books continue to empower, inspire and motivate people to aspire to a higher level of understanding through the written word.

Our company is dedicated to assisting those individuals who desire to publish Christian books that are uplifting, inspiring and self-help in nature. We also offer assistance for those who would like to self-publish.

The special service that we provide is customized, quality layout and design for every client. This gives every new author a chance at becoming successfully-published. For every book, we offer exposure and a worldwide presence to help the book and the author become discovered!

"As an author and publisher, I can guide you through the steps of creating, editing, proofreading and providing you with a professional layout and design for any printed item, one you'll be proud to call your own."

- Kathleen Schubitz

Founder and CEO

RPJ @ COMPANY, INC.

"Where quality and excellence meet face to face!"

www.store.rpjandco.com

CPSIA information can be obtained at www.ICGtesting.com
Printed in the USA
LVOW031932181211

259988LV00001B/10/P